Created AND Redeemed

Discovering God's Glorious Plan for Your Life

An Adult Faith Formation Program on
Pope John Paul II's Theology of the Body

Study Guide

by Christopher West

Abbreviations

CCC *Catechism of the Catholic Church*, Second Edition (Libreria Editrice Vaticana, 1997)

EA *Ecclesia in America*, John Paul II's Apostolic Exhortation on the Church in America (Pauline, 1999)

EV *Evangelium Vitae*, John Paul II's Encyclical Letter on the Gospel of Life (Pauline, 1995)

FC *Familiaris Consortio*, John Paul II's Apostolic Exhortation on the Christian Family (Pauline, 1981)

GS *Gaudium et Spes*, Vatican II's Pastoral Constitution on the Church in the Modern World (Pauline, 1965)

LF *Letter to Families*, John Paul II's Letter in the Year of the Family (Pauline, 1994)

LR *Love & Responsibility*, Karol Wojtyla's (John Paul II's) philosophical work on sexuality (Ignatius Press, 1993)

MD *Mulieris Dignitatem*, John Paul II's Apostolic Letter on the Dignity and Vocation of Women (Pauline, 1988)

TB *The Theology of the Body*, John Paul II's addresses on Human Love in the Divine Plan (Pauline 1997)*

VS *Veritatis Splendor*, John Paul II's encyclical letter on the Splendor of Truth (Pauline, 1993)

WH *Witness to Hope*, George Weigel's biography of Pope John Paul II (Harper Collins, 1999)

*For ease of reference, page numbers provided refer to this edition. However, please note that the 1997 one-volume edition of the Pope's catechesis was copyedited and may differ slightly from the original Vatican translation quoted in this study guide.

Other Resources by Christopher West

Books:
   Good News About Sex & Marriage: Answers to Your Honest Questions about Catholic Teaching (Servant, 2000)

   Crash Course in the Theology of the Body: A Study Guide (GIFT Foundation, 2002). Distributed by Luminous Media

   Theology of the Body Explained: A Commentary on John Paul II's 'Gospel of the Body' (Pauline, 2003)

Audio & Video Productions:
   Luminous Media is Christopher West's official distributor of audio and video presentations. Visit ChristopherWest.com or LuminousMedia.org for more information or call 800-376-0520.

For speaking engagements call 847-649-8222.

© 2003 by Christopher West
All rights reserved. This study guide may not be reproduced without permission from Luminous Media, LLC.

All Scripture quotations are taken from the Revised Standard Version of the Bible, copyright 1946, 1952, and 1971 by the Division of Christian Education of the National Council of Churches of Christ in the USA.

Table of Contents

Talk 1:
What is the Theology of the Body & Why Is It So Important?...............................1
Study Questions–Talk #1...5

ა

Talk 2:
The Creation & Redemption of Man and Woman..7
Study Questions–Talk #2...10

ა

Talk 3:
The Resurrection of the Body & the Heavenly Marriage.....................................13
Study Questions–Talk #3...16

ა

Talk 4:
The Sacrament of Marriage & the Language of Sexual Love..............................17
Study Questions–Talk #4...21

Talk 1:
What is the Theology of the Body & Why Is It So Important?

1. Sex & the Meaning of Existence

"Theology of the body" is the working title John Paul II gave to 129 short talks he delivered between September 1979 and November 1984. It is a biblical reflection on the meaning of the body, sex, and marital love. But it is crucial to realize that this is not only meant for the married.

> **1a.** What we learn is obviously "important in regard to marriage." However it "is equally essential ...for the understanding of man in general: for the ...self-comprehension of his being in the world" (TB, 352-353).

> **1b.** Though it focuses on sexual love, the theology of the body affords "the rediscovery of the meaning of the whole of existence, the meaning of life" (TB, 168).

Think how intertwined questions of sex are with the ultimate questions we ask about life:

- Where do I come from and why do I exist?
- What is the meaning of life and how do I live it?
- What is my ultimate destiny and how do I attain it?
- Why is there evil in the world and how do I overcome it?

> **1c.** The call to communion inscribed in our sexuality is "the fundamental element of human existence in the world" (TB, 16), "the foundation of human life" (EA, n. 46), and, hence, "the deepest substratum [foundation] of human ethics and culture" (TB, 163).

> **1d.** "It is an illusion to think we can build a true culture of human life if we do not ...accept and experience sexuality and love and the whole of life according to their true meaning and their close inter-connection" (EV, n. 97).

> **1e.** The "choices and the actions [of men and women] take on all the weight of human existence in the union of the two" (TB, 376).

If the task of the twentieth century was to rid itself of the Christian sexual ethic, the task of the twenty-first century must be to reclaim it. But the often repressive approach of previous generations of Christians is not going to suffice. We need a fresh approach that reveals the *beauty* of God's plan for sex and the *joy* of living it.

2. Understanding the Body as a "Theology"

People are used to religion emphasizing the spiritual realm. However, many people are unfamiliar, and sometimes even uncomfortable, with a religious emphasis on the body. For John Paul, this is a false split. The spirit certainly takes priority. Yet, as the *Catechism* teaches...

> **2a.** "As a being at once body and spirit, man expresses and perceives spiritual realities through physical signs and symbols" (CCC, n. 1146).

The human body is the original "sign" of the ultimate spiritual reality. It is from this perspective that John Paul wants to study the human body–not as biological organism, but as a *theology*.

- Christianity is the religion of the Word made flesh!
- God's mystery revealed in human flesh (theology *of the body*)–this is the very "logic" of Christianity.

> **2b.** "Through the fact that the Word of God became flesh the body entered theology ...through the main door" (TB, 89).

> **2c.** "The body, in fact, and it alone, is capable of making visible what is invisible: the spiritual and divine. It was created to transfer into the visible reality of the world, the mystery hidden since time immemorial in God, and thus to be a sign of it" (TB, 76).

3. God's Mystery & the Spousal Analogy

What is the mystery hidden in God that the body signifies? In a word–*communion*.

> **3a.** "God has revealed his innermost secret: God himself is an eternal exchange of love, Father, Son, and Holy Spirit, and he has destined us to share in that exchange" (CCC, n. 221).

Scripture uses many images to describe God's love. Each has its own valuable place. But the spousal image is used far more than any other.

- The Bible begins and ends with marriages–Adam-Eve and Christ-Church.
- Spousal theology looks to the nuptial "book ends" of Genesis and Revelation as a key for interpreting what lies between.

- Through the lens of the spousal analogy we learn that God's eternal plan is to "marry" us (see Hos 2:19).
- God wanted this eternal plan of love and communion to be so obvious to us that he stamped an image of it in our very being by creating us as male and female.

"'For this reason a man shall leave his father and mother and be joined to his wife, and the two shall become one flesh.' This is a great mystery, and I mean in reference to Christ and the church" (Eph 5:31-32).

3b. "The Church cannot therefore be understood ...unless we keep in mind the 'great mystery' ...expressed in the 'one flesh' [union] of marriage and the family" (LF, n. 19).

3c. Understanding the true meaning of the body and sexuality "concerns the entire Bible" ("TB, 249). It plunges us into "the perspective of the whole Gospel, of the whole teaching, in fact, of the whole mission of Christ" (TB, 175).

3d. "John Paul's portrait of sexual love as an icon of the interior life of God" is "one of the boldest reconfigurations of Catholic theology in centuries." It "has barely begun to shape the Church's theology, preaching, and religious education. When it does, it will compel a dramatic development of thinking about virtually every major theme in the Creed" (WH, 336, 853)

Like all analogies, the image of sexual love, while very helpful, is also limited and inadequate.

3e. "In no way is God in man's image. He is neither man nor woman. God is pure spirit in which there is no place for the difference between the sexes. But the respective 'perfections' of man and woman reflect something of the infinite perfection of God" (CCC, n. 370; see also nn. 42, 239).

3f. God's mystery "remains transcendent in regard to [the spousal] analogy as in regard to any other analogy, whereby we seek to express it in human language" (TB, 330). At the same time, however, there "is no other human reality which corresponds more, humanly speaking, to that divine mystery" (homily, 12/30/88).

4. Unmasking the Counterfeits

If given the choice between a real million dollar bill and a counterfeit, which would you prefer? But what if you were raised in a culture that incessantly bombarded you with propaganda convincing you that the counterfeit was the real thing?

- Satan seeks to counter God's plan by plagiarizing the sacraments (Tertullian).

NOTES

- That which is most sacred is that which is most often and most violently profaned.
- God's eternal plan for the body is union, communion, marriage; this brings life.
- Satan's counter-plan for the body is separation, fracture, divorce; this brings death.
- St. Paul's first words of advice in fighting the spiritual battle: "gird your loins with the truth" (Eph 6:14).

4a. Marriage and the family are "placed at the center of the great struggle between good and evil, between life and death, between love and all that is opposed to love" (LF, n. 23).

5. Structure of the Teaching

Through an in-depth reflection on the Scriptures John Paul seeks to answer two universal questions:
   (1) "What does it mean to be human?"
   (2) "How am I supposed to live my life in a way that brings true happiness?"

These questions frame the two main parts of the Pope's study. In turn, each of these two parts contains three "cycles" or subdivisions broken down as follows.

PART I: "What does it mean to be human?"

- Cycle 1: *Our Origin.* This concerns man's experience of the body and sex before sin. It's based on Christ's discussion with the Pharisees about God's plan for marriage "in the beginning" (see Mt 19:3-9).

- Cycle 2: *Our History.* This concerns man's experience of the body and sex affected by sin yet redeemed in Christ. It's based on Jesus' words in the Sermon on the Mount regarding adultery committed "in the heart" (see Mt 5: 27-28).

- Cycle 3: *Our Destiny.* This concerns man's experience of the body and sex in the resurrection. It's based on Christ's discussion with the Sadducees regarding the body's glorified state (see Mt 22: 23-33).

PART II: "How am I supposed to live my life in a way that brings true happiness?"

- Cycle 4: *Celibacy for the Kingdom.* This is a reflection on Christ's words about those who sacrifice marriage for the kingdom of heaven (see Mt 19:12).

- Cycle 5: *Christian Marriage*. This is primarily a reflection on St. Paul's grand "spousal analogy" in Ephesians 5.

- Cycle 6: *Sexual Morality & Procreation*. In light of his preceding analysis, John Paul shifts the discussion on sexual morality from legalism ("How far can I go before I break the law?") to liberty ("What's the truth of sexuality that sets me *free* to love?").

Study Questions–Talk #1
What is the Theology of the Body & Why Is It So Important?

Note: If your group discussion time is limited, we recommend you focus on questions 2, 4, 5, 6, 7, 8, 10, 12, 13, 14, 17, 19, 22 or select the questions that you think are most appropriate for your group.

1. Why do you think the Pope began his pontificate by emphasizing this deeper understanding of the human person and sexual love?
2. Why is this teaching for all people and not just for married couples?
3. Have you asked any of these four questions below? Have you found answers?
    - Where do I come from and why do I exist?
    - What is the meaning of life and how do I live it?
    - What is my ultimate destiny and how do I attain it?
    - Why is there evil in the world and how do I overcome it?
4. What is the effect of a culture's understanding of sexuality on the overall health of the culture?
5. What are some examples of humanity's attempts to build a culture without morals or without God? What has been the result?
6. What is your reaction to the following statement by Christopher West?
    "If the task of the twentieth century was to rid itself of the Christian sexual ethic, the task of the twenty-first century must be to reclaim it."
7. Have you seen in your own life or the life of others the "false split" of body and spirit that Christopher West spoke of? If so, which one was more emphasized and what were the ramifications?
8. How does the body make invisible things visible?

NOTES

9. Why do people often disdain their bodies rather than see God's beauty in them?
10. In what ways might the human family reflect or "image" the Trinity, the eternal family of Father, Son, and Holy Spirit?
11. What are the various images the Bible uses to describe God's love for us?
12. Why do you think the spousal image is used far more than any other?
13. According to the prophet Hosea, God wants to "marry" us (see Hosea 2:19). How does this make you feel?
14. In what ways might the husband/wife relationship reflect or image the relationship between Christ and the Church?
15. Which of these three statements by George Weigel most intrigues you and why?
    1. "John Paul's portrait of sexual love as an icon of the interior life of God" is "one of the boldest reconfigurations of Catholic theology in centuries." (WH, 336, 853)
    2. The theology of the body "has barely begun to shape the Church's theology, preaching, and religious education. When it does, it will compel a dramatic development of thinking about virtually every major theme in the Creed." (WH, 853)
    3. The theology of the body is "a kind of *theological time bomb* set to go off with dramatic consequences, perhaps in the twenty-first century" (WH, 343).
16. Why do human analogies always fall short of God's mystery?
17. What are some of the "counterfeits" we commonly accept in our culture?
18. Why do we often believe and pursue the counterfeits over the "real thing"?
19. What do you think Jesus would say to those who are pursuing counterfeit loves?
20. What are some examples of sacred things that are profaned in our culture?
21. What are the two universal questions that Pope John Paul II seeks to answer through the theology of the body?
22. Why is it important to look at our origin, history, and destiny in order to discover the meaning of our humanity?
23. What are the three "cycles" or subdivisions of the second question he asks, "How am I supposed to live my life in a way that brings true happiness?"

Talk 2:
The Creation & Redemption of Man and Woman

CYCLE 1: OUR ORIGIN

1. Christ Points us Back to "the Beginning"

"For your hardness of heart Moses allowed you to divorce your wives, but from the beginning it was not so" (Mt 19:8).

- By starting with Christ's words, the Pope makes a specific statement about our humanity.

- If our goal is to understand "who we are," we must turn to Christ.

1a. Christ "fully reveals man to himself and makes his supreme calling clear" (GS, n. 22).

1b. The "first man and the first woman must constitute ...the model ...for all men and women who, in any period, are united so intimately as to be 'one flesh'" (TB, 50).

2. Man is "Alone" in the World (Original Solitude)

"Then the Lord God said, 'It is not good that the man should be alone'" (Gen 2:18).

- This means not only that man is "alone" without the opposite sex, but that the human being (male and female) is "alone" in the visible world as a *person*.

- Adam realizes he is "different" from the animals. He's made in God's image. He has freedom – the capacity to *choose* between good and evil.

- Adam realizes his fundamental vocation: love of God and love of neighbor (see Lk 10:27).

- All this is experienced *in the body*.

2a. Based on the experience of his body, man "might have reached the conclusion … that he was substantially similar to the [animals]." Instead, "he reached the conviction that he was 'alone.'" (TB, 39)

2b. The "body expresses the person. It is, therefore, in all its materiality, almost penetrable and transparent, in such a way as to make it clear who man is (and who he should be)" (TB, 41).

3. Called to Live in Relationship (Original Unity)

Man "cannot fully find himself except through the sincere gift of himself" (GS, n. 24). "Therefore a man leaves his father and his mother and cleaves to his wife, and they become one flesh" (Gen 2:24).

- Their unity in "one flesh" is worlds apart from the copulation of animals. Unlike the animals, man and woman have the capacity to love (freedom).

- Therefore, like the experience of "solitude," unity also reveals that man and woman are created in God's image.

3a. Becoming "one flesh" refers not only to the joining of two bodies but is "a 'sacramental' expression which corresponds to the **communion of persons**" (TB, 123).

3b. "Man becomes the image of God not so much in the moment of solitude as in the moment of communion." In other words, man images God "not only through his own humanity, but also through the communion of persons which man and woman form right from the beginning.... On all this, right from the beginning, there descended the blessing of fertility linked with human procreation" (TB, 46).

4. Naked without Shame (Original Nakedness)

"And the man and his wife were both naked, and were not ashamed" (Gen 2:25).

- The Pope calls this the "key" for understanding God's original plan for man and woman (see TB, 52).

- They experienced sexual desire only as the desire to love in God's image. There is no shame (or fear) in love. "Perfect love casts out fear" (1 Jn 4:18).

4a. Nakedness reveals the **nuptial meaning of the body** which is the body's "capacity of expressing love: that love precisely in which the person becomes a gift and–by means of this gift–fulfills the very meaning of his being and existence" (TB, 63).

4b. "The fact that 'they were not ashamed' means that the woman was not an 'object' for the man nor him for her" (TB, 75). They "see and know each other, in fact, with all the peace of the interior gaze" (TB, 57).

4c. "'Nakedness' signifies the original good of God's vision. It signifies ...the 'pure' value of humanity as male and female, the 'pure' value of the body and of sex" (TB, 57).

4d. Original nakedness demonstrates that "holiness entered the visible world." It is "in his body as male or female [that] man feels he is a subject of holiness." Holiness is what "enables man to express himself deeply with his own body... precisely by means of the 'sincere gift' of himself" (TB, 76-77).

CYCLE 2: OUR HISTORY

5. Adultery in the Heart

"You have heard that it was said, 'You shall not commit adultery.' But I say to you that everyone who looks at a woman lustfully has already committed adultery with her in his heart" (Mt 5:27-28).

5a. "Are we to fear the severity of these words, or rather have confidence in their salvific...power?" (TB, 159).

5b. Christ's words are "an invitation to a pure way of looking at others, capable of respecting the spousal [or nuptial] meaning of the body" (VS, n. 15).

5c. The heritage of our hearts "is deeper than the sinfulness inherited, deeper than lust.... The words of Christ ...reactivate that deeper heritage and give it real power in man's life" (TB, 168).

6. The Entrance of Shame

When they disobeyed God "the eyes of both were opened, and they knew that they were naked; and they sewed fig leaves together and made themselves aprons. ...'I was afraid, because I was naked; and I hid myself" (Gen 3:7, 10).

- When God's love "died" in their hearts, sexual desire became inverted, self-seeking.
- Lust, therefore, is sexual desire void of God's love.
- Lust causes us almost to stoop back to the level of animals, yet we still know we are called to more–we're called to love.

6a. "Man is ashamed of his body because of lust. In fact, he is ashamed not so much of his body as precisely of lust" (TB, 116).

6b. Shame also has a positive meaning as "a natural *form of self-defense for the person* against the danger of descending or being pushed into the position of an object for sexual use" (LR, 182).

6c. Shame enters when man "realizes for the first time that his body has ceased drawing upon the power of the spirit, which raised him to the level of the image of God" (TB, 115).

6d. The 'heart' has become a battlefield between love and lust. The more lust dominates the heart, the less the [heart] experiences the nuptial meaning of the body" (TB, 126).

7. The Redemption of the Body & the "New Ethos"

We "groan inwardly as we wait for ...the redemption of our bodies" (Rom 8:23).

NOTES

- St. Paul vividly describes the interior battle we all experience between good and evil (see Rom 7).

- But he also speaks of the power of redemption at work within us which is able to do far more than we ever think or imagine (see Eph 3:20).

- Christ not only confirms the ethical demands of God's law, he proclaims the "new ethos" of the Gospel.

- *Ethos* refers to our inner-world of values, what attracts and repulses us.

7a. The "'redemption of the body' is expressed not only in the resurrection as victory over death. It is present also in Christ's words addressed to 'historical' man... when ...Christ called man to overcome [lust] even in the uniquely interior movements of the human heart" (TB, 301).

7b. "Christian ethos is characterized by a transformation of ...the human person, both man and woman, such as to express and realize the value of the body and sex according to the Creator's original plan" (TB, 163).

7c. "The new dimension of *ethos* is always connected with the ...'heart,' and with its liberation from 'lust'" (TB, 158).

7d. "The Law of the Gospel ...does not add new external precepts, but proceeds to reform the heart" (CCC, n. 1968). In "the Sermon on the Mount ...the Spirit of the Lord gives new form to our desires" (CCC, n. 2764).

☙

Study Questions–Talk #2
The Creations & Redemption of Man and Woman

Note: If your group discussion time is limited, we recommend you focus on questions 3, 4, 5, 7, 8, 11, 13, 18, 19, 22, 24, 25, 27 or select the questions that you think are most appropriate for your group.

1. Why does the Pope begin with this quote from St. Matthew's Gospel—"For your hardness of heart, Moses allowed you to divorce your wives, but from the beginning it was not so"? (Mt 19:8)
2. What do you understand the phrase "Christ fully reveals man to himself" to mean?
3. In what primary way did Adam realize that he was "different" from the animals?
4. One of the key teachings of Vatican II states that "man cannot fully find himself except through the sincere gift

of self." What do you understand the Church to mean by this statement?

5. Becoming "one flesh" refers to much more than the joining of two bodies. Why?
6. Traditional theology has stated that we image God as individuals through our rational soul. Although this is true, John Paul II has gone deeper to explain that we also image God through the _____ of persons.
7. Why does John Paul II consider nakedness without shame as the "key" to understanding God's original plan for man and woman?
8. Why were Adam and Eve not ashamed in their nakedness prior to the Fall?
9. How did Adam and Eve experience sexual desire prior to the Fall?
10. What does "nuptial" mean? What other words could be used to describe the phrase, "nuptial meaning of the body"?
11. Why do we instinctively seem to cover ourselves if a stranger were to enter into a room and see us unclothed?
12. Although the body is good and holy, why is it appropriate that we cover ourselves in a fallen world?
13. Why is it difficult to believe that our bodies are holy?
14. What did their original nakedness signify?
15. Why does the Pope choose this verse below to begin the section where he discusses "man in history"?

    "You have heard that it was said, 'You shall not commit adultery.' But I say to you that everyone who looks at a woman lustfully has already committed adultery with her in his heart" (Mt 5:27-28).

16. Why does the Pope say we should not fear the severity of Christ's words about lust?
17. Have you ever heard that Christ gives us "real power" to experience sexuality as the desire to love as God loves? Do you believe this?
18. How did sexual desire change after the fall?
19. Lust is sexual desire devoid of _____.
20. The Pope states that man becomes ashamed of his body because of _____.
22. The Pope said in his book *Love and Responsibility* that shame also has a positive meaning or result. What is this positive result?
23. What is St. Paul referring to when he says we "groan inwardly as we wait for...the redemption of our bodies" in Romans (8:23)?

NOTES

24. What does "ethos" mean?
25. Do you believe your ethos can actually change?
26. The *Catechism of the Catholic Church* says that the "Law of the Gospel...does not add new external precepts (i.e., laws), but proceeds to _____ the heart."
27. Why do most people think of Christian morality as an oppressive list of rules? What is "freedom from the law?"

Talk 3:
The Resurrection of the Body & the Heavenly Marriage

CYCLE 3: OUR DESTINY

1. Christ Points us to the Future

"For in the resurrection they neither marry nor are given in marriage" (Mt 22:30).

- Marriage exists only as a sign that's meant to point us to heaven, to the "Marriage of the Lamb" (Rev 19:7).

- In the resurrection, the sacrament will give way to the divine reality.

- This means the union of the sexes is not man's end-all-and-be-all. It's only an "icon."

- When we loose sight of our destiny, the *icon* inevitably becomes an *idol*.

1a. "Marriage and procreation ...did not determine definitively the original and fundamental meaning of being ...male and female. Marriage and procreation merely give a concrete reality to that meaning in ...history" (TB, 247).

2. The Beatific Vision

"For now we see in a mirror dimly, but then face to face" (1 Co 13:12).

- The beatific vision was foreshadowed (dimly, of course) right from the beginning in the union of man and woman.

- In the beatific vision, God will give himself totally to man, and we will respond with the total gift of ourselves to him.

2a. In "the resurrection we discover – in an [eternal] dimension – the same... nuptial meaning of the body ...in the meeting with the mystery of the living God ...face to face" (TB, 243).

2b. The beatific vision is "a concentration of knowledge and love on God himself." This knowledge "cannot be other than full participation in the interior life of God, that is, in the very Trinitarian reality" (TB, 244).

2c. This "will be a completely new experience." Yet "at the same time it will not be alienated in any way from what man took part in from 'the beginning' nor from what, in the historical dimension [concerned] the procreative meaning of the body and sex" (TB, 248).

2d. "In the joys of their love [God gives spouses] here on earth a foretaste of the wedding feast of the Lamb" (CCC, n. 1642).

2e. The Church "longs to be united with Christ, her Bridegroom, in the glory of heaven" where she "will rejoice one day with [her] Beloved, in a happiness and rapture that can never end" (CCC, n. 1821).

3. The Communion of Saints

"There are many parts, yet one body" (1 Cor 12:20).

- The Communion of Saints is the definitive expression of the human call to communion.

- It's the unity in "one body" of all who respond to the wedding invitation of the Lamb (see Rev 19).

- We will see all and be seen by all. We will know all and be known by all. And God will be "all in all" (Eph 1:23).

3a. "*For man*, this consummation will be the final realization of the unity of the human race, which God willed from creation. ...Those who are united with Christ will form the community of the redeemed, 'the holy city' of God, 'the Bride, the wife of the Lamb'" (CCC, n. 1045).

CYCLE 4: CHRISTIAN CELIBACY

4. Eunuchs "for the Kingdom"

Some "have made themselves eunuchs for the sake of the kingdom of heaven" (Mt 19:12).

- A eunuch is someone physically incapable of sexual relations.

- A eunuch "for the kingdom" is someone who freely forgoes sexual relations in order to devote all of his energies and desires to the union that alone can satisfy.

- Those who are celibate for the kingdom "skip" the sacrament in anticipation of the ultimate reality, the "Marriage of the Lamb."

- In this way they boldly proclaim that "the kingdom of God is here."

4a. Christ's words "clearly indicate the importance of the personal choice and also the ...particular grace" of this vocation (TB, 263).

4b. In the Latin Church, priests "are normally chosen from among men of faith who live a celibate life and who intend to remain celibate 'for the sake of the kingdom of heaven'" (CCC, n. 1579).

5. Christian Celibacy Flows from the Redemption of Sexuality

Without understanding the call to redemption, we inevitably look at marriage as a legitimate "outlet" for lust and at celibacy as hopelessly repressive.

- Christ calls *everyone* to experience "liberation from lust" through the redemption of the body.

- Only through this liberation do the Christian vocations (celibacy *and* marriage) make sense.

- Without this liberation, choosing celibacy for one's entire life is seen as absurd. With it, not only does it become possible; it becomes quite attractive.

5a. "Adultery in the heart is committed not only because man 'looks' in this way at a woman who is not his wife.... Even if he looked in this way at his wife, he could likewise commit adultery 'in his heart'" (TB, 157).

5b. The celibate must submit "the sinfulness of his [fallen] nature to the forces that spring from the mystery of the redemption of the body ...just as any other man does" (TB, 275).

6. Christian Celibacy Expresses the Nuptial Meaning of the Body

We cannot escape the nuptial meaning of our bodies without doing violence to our humanity.

- Celibacy *is not* a rejection of sexuality, but a living out of the deepest meaning of sexuality – union with Christ and his Church (see Eph 5:31-32).

- Every man is called in some way to be both a husband and a father.

- Every woman is called in some way to be both a wife and a mother.

6a. On "the basis of the same nuptial meaning of [the] body ...there can be formed the love that commits man to marriage for the whole duration of his life, but there can be formed also the love that commits man to a life of continence 'for the sake of the kingdom of heaven'" (TB, 284). Celibacy for the kingdom "has acquired the significance of an act of nuptial love" (TB, 282).

6b. The celibate person "has the knowledge of being able ...to fulfill himself 'differently' and, in a certain way, 'more' than through matrimony, becoming a 'true gift to others'" (TB, 274).

NOTES

Created & Redeemed – Page 16

Study Questions–Talk #3
The Resurrection of the Body & the Heavenly Marriage

Note: If your group discussion time is limited, we recommend you focus on questions 1, 2, 5, 8, 9, 10, 11, 13, 14 or select the questions that you think are most appropriate for your group.

1. What is your initial reaction to Christ's teaching that there will be no marriage in heaven?
2. What does human marriage point to in the eternal realm?
3. Christopher West posits that when we lose sight of our destiny (i.e. communion with God in heaven), we can make the sexual relationship (which is just the icon or "image" of the heavenly marriage to come) an idol that is worshipped. If this is true, how can this have an effect on marriages or even dating relationships?
4. What is the Beatific Vision?
5. How was the Beatific Vision foreshadowed right from the beginning in the union of man and woman?
6. What particular light does the theology of the body shed on the communion of saints?
7. What is a "eunuch for the Kingdom"?
8. Why does the world generally scorn celibacy?
9. How is it that celibacy foreshadows the Kingdom of God in heaven?
10. What are the supernatural reasons (versus the temporal benefits) for a celibate priesthood?
11. Does the world see marriage as a legitimate outlet for lust? If so, what might be the ramifications of this?
12. How does this view of "redeemed sexuality" (where our ethos is actually changed towards that which is true and good) affect your view of celibacy?
13. How can someone commit "adultery in the heart" with his or her own spouse?
14. Why is celibacy not a rejection of sexuality, but a living out of the deepest meaning of sexuality, according Pope John Paul II?
15. How is every man called in some way to be a husband and father?
16. How is every woman called in some way to be both a wife and mother?

Talk 4:
The Sacrament of Marriage & the Language of Sexual Love

CYCLE 5: CHRISTIAN MARRIAGE

1. Mutual Submission

"Be subject to one another out of reverence for Christ. As the church is subject to Christ, so let wives also be subject in everything to their husbands. Husbands, love your wives, as Christ loved the church and gave himself up for her" (Eph 5: 21, 24-25).

- According to the analogy, the wife is a symbol of the Church and the husband is a symbol of Christ.

- Christ came not to *be* served *but to serve*–to lay down his life for his Bride (see Mt 20:28).

- St. Paul *does not justify male domination*. This is the result of sin (see Gen 3:16).

- St. Paul is seeking to restore the original order *before* sin.

1a. Since the "submission of the Church to Christ ...consists in experiencing his love," we can conclude that "the wife's 'submission' to her husband [also] ...signifies above all 'the experiencing of love'" (TB, 320).

1b. "So therefore that 'reverence for Christ' and 'respect' of which [St. Paul] speaks, is none other than a spiritually mature form of that mutual attraction: man's attraction to femininity and woman's attraction to masculinity" (TB, 379).

1c. If a husband is truly to love his wife, "it is necessary to insist that intercourse must not serve merely as a means of allowing [his] climax. ...The man must take [the] difference between male and female reactions into account ...so that climax may be reached [by] both ...and as far as possible occur in both simultaneously." The husband must do this "not for hedonistic, but for altruistic reasons." In this case, if "we take into account the shorter and more violent curve of arousal in the man, [such] tenderness on his part in the context of marital intercourse acquires the significance of an act of virtue" (LR, 272, 275).

2. The Language of the Body

"'For this reason a man shall leave his father and mother and be joined to his wife, and the two shall become one flesh.'

This is a great mystery, and I mean in reference to Christ and the church" (Eph 5:21-33).

- The body has a "language" that's meant to proclaim the truth of God's love poured out in Christ's body "given up" for us.

- Christ's love is *free, total, faithful,* and *fruitful.*

- This is precisely what spouses commit to at the altar, and what they are meant to express when they become "one flesh."

- Intercourse, therefore, is where the words of the wedding vows *become flesh.*

2a. The "very words 'I take you to be my wife–my husband' ...can be fulfilled only by means of conjugal intercourse." Here "we pass to the reality which corresponds to these words" (TB, 355).

2b. "As ministers of a sacrament which is constituted by consent and perfected by conjugal union, man and woman are called to express that mysterious 'language' of their bodies in all the truth which is proper to it. By means of gestures and reactions, by means of the whole dynamism ...of tension and enjoyment–whose direct source is the body in its masculinity and its femininity, the body in its action and interaction–by means of all this, ...the person, 'speaks.' ...Precisely on the level of this 'language of the body' ...man and woman reciprocally express themselves in the fullest and most profound way possible to them" (TB, 397-398).

3. The Body is "Prophetic"

A prophet is one who proclaims the mystery of God. We must be careful to distinguish between true and false prophets (see TB, 365).

- If we can speak the truth with our bodies, we can also speak lies.

- Who is it that might want us to speak *lies* with our bodies?

3a. Sexual union is a "test of life and death." Spouses, "becoming one as husband and wife, find themselves in the situation in which the powers of good and evil fight and compete against each other" (TB, 376).

CYCLE 6: SEXUAL MORALITY & PROCREATION

4. Living as True Prophets

"This is my commandment, that you love one another as I have loved you" (Jn 15:12).

- All questions of sexual morality come down to one basic question: Is the act an authentic sign of God's *free, total, faithful, fruitful* love or is it not?

- Practically speaking, how healthy would a marriage be if husbands and wives were regularly unfaithful to their wedding vows?

4a. We "can speak of moral good and evil" in the sexual relationship "according to whether ...or not it has the character of the truthful sign" (TB, 141-142).

4b. The language of the body has "clear-cut meanings" all of which are "'programmed' ...in the conjugal consent." For example, to "the question: 'Are you willing to accept responsibly and with love the children that God may give you...?'"–the man and the woman reply: 'Yes'" (TB, 363, 364).

4c. Those who live the "ethos of redemption" experience "a salvific fear ...of violating or degrading what bears in itself the sign of the divine mystery of creation and redemption" (TB, 416).

5. Responsible Parenthood

It is a myth that the Church teaches couples are obligated to have as many children as is physically possible. The Church calls couples to a *responsible* exercise of parenthood.

5a. Those "are considered 'to exercise responsible parenthood who prudently and generously decide to have a large family, or who, for serious reasons and with due respect to the moral law, choose to have no more children for the time being or even for an indeterminate period'" (TB, 394).

So, what could a couple do if they had a "serious reason" to avoid a child that would not violate the meaning of intercourse as a sign of God's love?

5b. The difference between contraception and periodic abstinence "is much wider and deeper than is usually thought, one which involves in the final analysis two irreconcilable concepts of the human person and of human sexuality" (FC, n. 32).

6. A Question of Faith

Many object that the Church's teaching doesn't correspond to our real possibilities.

- We must be careful not to fall into the trap of "holding the form of religion" while "denying the power of it" (2 Tim 3:5).

- It's a question of faith: do we believe that Christ can empower us to love as he loves or do we not? Is redemption a sham?

6a. What "are the 'concrete possibilities of man'? And of which man are we speaking? Of man *dominated* by lust or of man *redeemed by Christ*? This is what is at stake: the *reality* of Christ's redemption. *Christ has redeemed us!* This means He has given us the possibility of realizing the *entire truth* of our being; He has set our freedom free from the *domination* of [lust]. And if redeemed man still sins, this is not due to an imperfection of Christ's redemptive act, but to man's will not to avail himself of the grace which flows from that act" (VS, n. 103).

❧

Study Questions–Talk #4
The Sacrament of Marriage & the Language of Sexual Love

Note: If your group discussion time is limited, we recommend you focus on questions 1, 2, 5, 6, 8, 10, 13, 14, 15, 16, 17, 18, 19, 21 or select the questions that you think are most appropriate for your group.

1. How is the wife a symbol of the Church and the husband a symbol of Christ?
2. Why do people react so negatively to the verse in Ephesians 5 that speaks of wives being "submissive?"
3. How does the Pope explain this spousal "submission" passage in his theology of the body?
4. What do couples commit to at the altar?
5. How is Christ's love for us *free, total, faithful,* and *fruitful*?
6. How is a married couple's love *free, total, faithful,* and *fruitful*?
7. Are children the only expression of "fruitfulness" in marriage?
8. How do people speak "truth" with their bodies as well as "lies"?
9. John Paul said the following statements: *Sexual union is a "test of life and death." Spouses, "becoming one as husband and wife, find themselves in the situation in which the powers of good and evil fight and compete against each other"* (TB, 376). Do you think these statements are an exaggeration?
10. What is the one question that helps determine the morality of a sexual act?
11. Have you experienced a genuine change in ethos in areas of your moral or married life?
12. Does the Church expect us to have as many children as possible in marriage?

13. What do you understand the Church to teach in the area of marital love and openness to children?
14. What could a couple do if they had a "serious reason" to avoid a child that wouldn't violate the meaning of intercourse as a sign of God's love?
15. How does abstaining from fertile intercourse differ from sterilizing intercourse through contraception?
16. Most people look at contraception as simply a means of avoiding pregnancy. What are some of the unintended consequences of contraception on marriage and society?
17. Why do many people tend to think the Church is "out of touch" when it comes to sexual morality?
18. Christ came not to condemn, but to save (see Jn 3:17). The authentic teaching of the Church always reflects this. How, then, is the Church's teaching on sexual morality a message of salvation?
19. What role do you think John Paul II's theology of the body has in building a culture of life?
20. In light of this introductory course, do you believe that George Weigel's statements below are (a) absolutely true, (b) generally true, (c) partially true, or (d) not true at all? Please explain your reasoning.
    1. "John Paul's portrait of sexual love as an icon of the interior life of God" is "one of the boldest reconfigurations of Catholic theology in centuries."
    2. The Theology of the Body "has barely begun to shape the Church's theology, preaching, and religious education. When it does, it will compel a dramatic development of thinking about virtually every major theme in the Creed"
    3. The Theology of the Body is "a kind of *theological time bomb* set to go off with dramatic consequences, ...perhaps in the twenty-first century" (WH, 343).
21. How has participating in this study affected you?

In Conclusion...

7. The New Sexual Revolution

If the future of humanity passes by way of marriage and the family (see FC, n. 86), the future of marriage and the family passes by way of the Pope's theology of the body.

- There will be no renewal of the Church and of the world without a renewal of marriage and the family.

- There will be no renewal of marriage and the family without a return to the full truth of God's plan for the body and sexuality.

- But this will not happen without a fresh proposal that compellingly demonstrates to the modern world how the Christian sexual ethic—far from the cramped, prudish list of prohibitions it's assumed to be—is a liberating message of *salvation* that corresponds perfectly with the desires of the human heart.

The Pope's theology of the body has already begun a sexual counter-revolution. It is spreading and it can't be stopped.

> **7a.** The theology of the body is "a kind of *theological time bomb* set to go off with dramatic consequences, ...perhaps in the twenty-first century" (WH, 343).

I appeal to you: make it your mission in life to know and live the true meaning of your body. This is not a footnote in the Christian life:

> **7b.** Understanding God's plan for the body and sexuality plunges us into "the perspective of the whole Gospel, of the whole teaching, in fact, of the whole mission of Christ" (TB, 175).

If we live this good news—this "gospel of the body"—and share it with everyone we know, we shall not fall short of renewing the face of the earth.

Acknowledgements

Created & Redeemed Study Guide written by Christopher West. *Created & Redeemed Study Guide* questions written by Matthew Pinto and Christopher West.

Sponsored by the Order of Malta and the Cincinnati Chapter of Malta

The *Order of Malta* is a lay religious order of the Catholic Church founded in 1099. The Knights and Dames fo Malta have two historical charisms: the witness of the faith and service to the poor and sick. The order is international and chapters are found in most major cities in the world.

NOTES

NOTES

NOTES

NOTES

NOTES

NOTES